hope is a traveler

c✕つ

"These are beautiful, holy, wise and inspired poems by a soul that has suffered deeply and rejoiced deeply. Buy and savor this book." —ANDREW HARVEY, author of *The Hope, Radical Passion, A Journey in Ladakh*

"With a penetrating eye and in a tender, intimate voice, Susan Frybort illuminates in these poems the gossamer beauty of our every-day life." —ROGER HOUSDEN, author of *Ten Poems to Change Your Life, For Lovers of God Everywhere*

"A ticket to wonder. *Hope Is A Traveler* invites the reader to climb aboard a caravan of love as it meanders through moments of loss and infinite joy in the life of its author. Daring to bare the innermost core of her pain, as well as the exalted way of human interaction and Spirit guidance, Susan Frybort's words, in my mind, sit in harmony with her historical poetic compatriots of Rumi, Hafiz and Gibran. Her experiences are both unique and universal and the reader can immerse in the Divinely Human and Humanly Divine nature of her soul spilling over onto what she calls 'the heart road.' Travel well." —EDIE WEINSTEIN, LSW, *Vivid Life* radio host, author of *The Bliss Mistress Guide To Transforming the Ordinary Into the Extraordinary*

"Susan Frybort is a highly intelligent and skilful free verse Poetess who probes difficult human questions with skill and perspicuity, in a most attractive and very readable way. In addition, her personal findings could well help resolve many of the dilemmas that readers may meet in their own lives." —ALAN JACOBS, Poet Writer Author, President *Ramana Maharshi Foundation UK*

"These poems by Susan Frybort are personal reflections on the nature of spirit and the ways in which objective reality and spiritual awareness intersect. Frybort writes attentively and with a sense of gratitude and reverence. There is much thoughtfulness and a gentle intelligence in these poems that lead readers through a portal of hope toward deeper understanding of self and spirit." —ADELE KENNY, Poetry Editor, *Tiferet Journal*

"In this wonderful book, Susan Frybort displays the uncovering of the heart. She reminds us of the heart's healing potential, while exploring what might hold the mind at bay. She unearths the root of that which keeps our happiness entranced with a longing for fulfillment. And she does it all with such grace and loving kindness. We really enjoyed her beautiful poems, and felt her heart within ours." —STEPHEN AND ONDREA LEVINE, coauthors of *Embracing the Beloved, Who Dies?, The Healing I Took Birth For*

"Susan Frybort's work is true poetry. She skillfully conveys central human concerns with apparent ease: love, pain, suffering, hope, empathy, and all the other truths, feelings and emotions that make life worth living. More, her words are imbued with a special potency that allow her readers to feel feelings and experience experiences that they might otherwise not be privy to. Few poets can work this magic, but she does, easily, effectively. To experience this phenomenon, one has to actually read her work. One final point: Although she rarely delves into spiritual subjects directly, all of her work has an intense spiritual dimension, speaking to parts of the soul that are dying to hear her message." —STEVEN J. ROSEN, author of *Hidden Glory of India, The Yoga of Kirtan*, and assorted books on Eastern thought and Hindu philosophy

"Reading this collection of poems, I saw so much of my own life's journey mirrored in their beautifully crafted words. The years of dissatisfaction with myself, even at times self-hatred, learned from a society that doesn't let us simply be just the way we find ourselves but always wants us to be somehow different—it's all so poignantly reflected here. My decades in religion, then later "spirituality," all of them an attempt to address my perceived inadequacy—my days of stormy, "darkened clouds, watering down and dampening my dreams," as I fought the fight my upbringing taught me against living like "a cornflower—somewhere in a morning field, far away from here—singing out to the sky's vermillion sunrise, with not a care in the world." Until, at last, I began to awaken to the central insight of these poems, that my humanness isn't something to be endlessly apologized for, but that "God's divinity and my humanness are the same." You'll want to read slowly, to ponder, to simply sit with the rich metaphors, the deep insights, the heartfelt wonder these images evoke." —DAVID ROBERT ORD, author of *Your Forgotten Self*, coauthor of *The Coming Interspiritual Age*, and author and narrator of the audiobook *Lessons in Loving—A Journey into the Heart*

"Opening, soothing, nourishing, lightening. This is a book to keep close to your heart! It will open you to the re-membering that brings us home." —MARY O'MALLEY, author of *What's in the Way IS the Way*

hope is a traveler

a collection of poems

S̲USAN F̲RYBORT

ENREALMENT PRESS
TORONTO, CANADA

Published by Enrealment Press
PO Box 64
Acton, Ontario
Canada L7J 2M2

Cover photo by Ollyy/Shutterstock
Author photos by Lindsay Knapp
Cover and book design by Allyson Woodrooffe (go-word.com)
Printed in the USA

Library and Archives Canada Cataloguing in Publication

Frybort, Susan, 1966-, author
    Hope is a traveler /Susan Frybort.

Poems.
Issued in print and electronic formats.
ISBN 978-0-9808859-7-2 (pbk.).--ISBN 978-0-9808859-8-9 (pdf)
    I. Title.

PS3606.R93H66 2015   811'.6   C2015-900263-X
                                         C2015-900264-8

Dedicated to Lindsay Taylor,
the courage in my heart.

And for you, Lorne and Lily.

Contents

hope is a traveler

Empathy

Today I woke feeling my ordinariness next to me.
I never wrote a masterpiece,
painted the perfect landscape,
or played an etude.
I cannot beat the African healing drum like a shaman
to intercede between the realms.
I don't know how to touch people
to resolve them of all their inner conflict or traumas.
I never looked into a crystal and saw the divine,
I'm not a psychologist,
a therapist, a counselor or a saint.
And Das is not part of my name—
my name is ordinary.
As I thought about how the opportunity
to tend to a painful wound,
as if it were an injured plant,
or delicately administer soothing salve
to another earthly soul
would not be mine because I do not possess
the official requirements,
I felt a particular sadness,
as though I were, somehow, not enough.

Then suddenly I remembered
everything is well within me.

For I know that all my certainties
and all that has ever been established before me
are in sacred correspondence.
I know about the stars
and how they gather as constellations
to guide the wanderer through all the eras.
I know of the bamboo that will not flower
until many years pass by,
and how the blossom gives its life
as nourishment and protection
so that the tiny seedling within
may push forward and grow.
I know there are mysteries not fully understood.
I know each life holds a unique path,
eventually drawing to an end for all—
and when I sat at the bedside
of an elderly woman dying,
or on my knees next to a fading animal
struggling for her last breaths
after a long earthly journey,
there was no difference in my attentiveness.
I felt equal compassion for both,
then wept the same mournful tears.

And I know for certain, that when I look
into another human being—
whether they have eyes to see or not—
I can behold them.
I can view the hurt in them, and feel the wounds in me.
It is a pain that agonizes quietly inside as we share it,
so I reach out to comfort them.
These are the opportunities to extend
and touch another soul with all that is in me now.
And that is good enough for me.

River of Love

When like the sudden wind
on the ocean,
the tides of life washed me ashore—
you collected my heart among the remnants,
then breathed deeply
into all my quiet dreams.

O river of love,
streaming out from my soul—
how can I ever swim back to before?

Blending Pulses

Feel it and be still,
there is no mystic secret.
Like the rhythm of the rain,
each vein of our being—
blending pulses.

Ancient Moon

I hid my soul
in perfect silence
amid the eventide,
unseen and unknown,
the only beam
a ghost of myself.
How is it that a life could pale away suddenly?
Seems the only thing I could count on
were the phases of an aging moon—
predictable, yet vital.
Seems the only thing I crave now
is an opening outside the shadows
to exist unobscured,
waxing full
and unrestricted,
like a living,
ancient moon.

Ordinary Day

There is nothing commonplace about a sunrise,
where all of life breathes into a fresh dawning.
There's nothing trite about the day-to-day routine
when your thoughts ascend then rest upon
the preciousness of life,
and bask in the warmth of that wonder.
You become alive to each ordinary day,
electing to see the supernatural in the familiar—
the winding road meeting up with another,
the leaves that mingle on the wind together,
and the children laughing in the next room, at play.
Those who chose to experience breath
in this blessed existence,
arise to the true miracle of living—seeing one another
for who they are right now, in this passing time,
in these present hours.
We are many paths of one accord—extending,
connecting and exchanging.
Inhaling, resting then exhaling—
continually entwined in a ritual
of spiritual communion with one another.

And it is this life that becomes a living,
breathing prayer
reaching out to the entire world.

Inside I Am You

That which was in me
hidden and sound,
I searched for—
all the while
in me
I found.
Freely I give,
begotten and began
was me,
and that I am—
you are me
inside I am you.

Dreams

I walked alone for a while—
the stars were silent in that time,
as all my soul's confessions
seemed to wane into a sliver.
And when the bygone visions born of long ago
made a pact to search for me,
then carry me back to remembrance,
I could fondly recall their hopeful impressions
overlaying all my uncertainty—
like lily vines guarding its forgotten castle—
recurring like some woven mist-dream,
yet palpable
and true.

I Will Not Forget You

I will not forget you,
you are written beautiful and lasting
in my mind evermore.
I will not forget you,
your heart revolves around the sun,
seen as light that has blessed
each day that is born.
I will not forget you.
Held in my memory,
our shared hours, treasured—
now in heaven's infinite hands you rest.
I will not forget you, soul.
Though you shine in other realms tonight,
I see the ray of eternal grace you brought
to this thankful, fleeting life
in this momentary world.

Salamander

Resting in springtime's
sugary grass,
the sun lulls me
into an afternoon's sleep—
a lone salamander
who managed her way out
from under the night's cold rock
and into day.
Just then, a shrill voice
broke me,
quite suddenly.
Startled, I cry with dry eyes
and thin skin—
to my surprise I grow new limbs,
then scale
the tallest
white aspen.

Enlightenment

I broke from the tightest shoot
upon an obscure branch
to declare my imparting,
and stretch my reaching tendril.
Ever climbing and illuminating
inside my newest knowledge,
born in aurora to see the light that day,
then folding close as the sun grows dim—
arising once more to start over again.

And the spiritual ones who say
they have already arrived—
extending from their highest point,
their eyes always open—
unheeding the cusp,
never hailing the morning.
Can't they see the destination in me?
I am the present journey
where the end becomes the dawning.

Broken Waves

As life crests and steepens,
our pain finds its way to the shore—
broken waves we are to the very end,
yet the sea can't hold all we've perfected.

Glowing Embers

Our fire,
flaming wildly at first kiss,
always remembers
within its forever tryst—
rekindling time,
smoldering ageless,
we find
a wondrous paradise
still simmering
inside
those glowing embers.

Sweet Whimsy

I like to walk barefoot in the morning grass—
fresh wet blades tickling my skin
like tender wings
or the flitter of a soft tongue.
My mind,
tiptoeing around your
sweet whimsy,
steps lightly with fascination.
And my thoughts on you, like my feet,
want to playfully dance
and wander.

We Break

We break.
We break and mend,
we flow—
against the surf
we fold.
We bend and twist,
we splay,
with undulated sway.
We break again,
and again, we mend—
along with the tide we land.
Our names are carved within our hearts
and etched upon the sand—
we break, we mend
like curling waves,
we wash up on
the strand.

Fly Away Tomorrow

Veranda sits wide open
again this early evening.
The dove's mournful call
floats on the breeze,
then gently into me—
all of the outside pouring in.
Packing cherished
longings tonight,
to fly away tomorrow—
and like a dove, I think,
no one will ever notice.

As Stars

I sit on the surface each day to the next, not always
going to that deep level if I can help it.
I would have to say, dipping in for a moment,
there has got to be
more to this—and just what is it—and why
do we all keep grasping for more?
I think in the end it could be said,
we all wanted the same.
We all wanted to be lights.
We all just want to be seen.
No matter the length we're to shine,
in that time we all yearn to be known.

So I see you, my star, just as you are.

Never Enough Septembers

When I awoke
to find you
at my side
one September morning,
my heart near yours
split open wide
and spilled
a wondrous joy
that washed away
our partings,
then filled the evenings
with a love so tender—
there could never, ever
be enough
Septembers.

Forsythia

Let the snow
where it falls,
cold and drift
the stolid soil.

Let the wind
its shivering cry,
bare in time
this wintered guise.

Well inside their
dormant sleep,
limpid memories
stem from me—

beams of golden
breath alive,
my forsythia's hope,
my Spring.

Wingless Beings

Lover of God
with me,
I saw the divine in thee—
though wingless beings,
we soar the wind,
into eternity.

Jaded Dusk

When all the seams came undone
and I stood alone in my affliction,
you arrived in time as sweet ointment,
then tenderly kissed my disease.
Sorrowful in my weakness, still, I looked to see a truth
within the calm of your placid eyes undisturbed,
a gift long awaited.

I remember us. We fell once before then climbed
the mighty summit. Clinging together,
our hearts shared a new pulse,
our desires woven and knitted closely—
we tumbled together
down a grassy hill,
staining our hearts with one another's love pledges.

And when your interest suddenly wandered past me,
I sang with my heart
and its crestfallen rhythms.
What made you lean in another direction?
As our connection began to fade
with heavens gentle colors,
I wept in early mourning.

I couldn't reach you to find passage
to an understanding.
I couldn't find you because you were on another plane,
I could not tell you. You were on a different
level of another ship,
steadily drifting from my wanting cries.
Like the sun sinking into the shadowy earth,
ignoring the sky's seductive pleading to stay,
you left me
colored with uncertainty,
as jaded dusk.

So I, holding onto the memory of your
hand in mine, breathe with resolving strength—
each breath emanating hope for your return,
your voice yet a soft murmur
in my ear, like many whispers—
your kiss a sealed promise upon my lips.

And I remember us.

The Robe

I could never claim to possess the ultimate insight.
The best I can do is to bide openly,
and listen for an understanding
to arrive in its due time.
I am not here to challenge and change you,
or dazzle you with otherworldly wisdom.
What can I tell you that you don't already
know about your deepest realm?
If I were to draw you out on clean paper
with lead and charcoal—
each light and shadow—
it would not do you justice, this rendering of mine.
I can say, I truly see you every now and then.
I see what lies within your soul—
the fearful apprehensions and agitation,
the hurt that lingers after suffering,
the hope within your scars,
and the determination that sits vigil
beside your doubts, unremitting.
I can see that your teardrops wet the soil
upon the path you walk,
and that nothing was ever in vain—
not the indifference you endured,
nor anyone's disdain.
You carry a burden for the world and its inhabitants
along with a tender sorrow as you recall
those who have gone on,
and remembering what you once had.

Nevertheless, it has all been stored up
to be exchanged as inspiration
within your many gifts and creations.
Surrounding all of this, I see your resolve
to search for meaning—while
your soul releases the light of forgiveness,
your heart holds on to love
in its many changing forms.

And then I can see it.
It is a cloth woven with the finest
of threads by toiling hands
to be made into the very garment
you will wear infinitely.
The wisdom of gold intertwined with the strength
from leaves of raffia palm, rustic and regal.
You have fashioned a robe
and this is the magnificence you wear and walk in.
It is unparalleled while enduring,
this cloak, interwoven
with all of life's pain and celebration.

Soon everything becomes crystalline before me
as all my misgivings fall away, I understand this:
Love is a security that cannot be denied,
an assurance that holds
no conditions nor clings to enmity.
It is a robe that blankets, woven over time
from delicate circumstance by arriving souls
set to course on truthful journeys,
then departing into timelessness,
wrapped safely in this everlasting mantle
of purest love.

Faith

Each day they stroll past and rarely notice me,
hidden among the obvious, walking close
within each journey.
Do you want to know who I am?
I am a bridge,
a mountain,
a leap into the dark unknown.
I am that drifting cloud you see,
on its way to a new home.

Bridge

Your eyes of gentle diamond gaze, at first I saw you,
miles away—between our rippling laughter,
you touched my quiet heart.
The bridge that stood before us was
both grand and daring, yet
I journeyed close. And once thereupon,
my bold, intrepid spirit
lifts to soar forever unwavering.
As I step onto each leaf, will you
meet me before the chasm?
How often had I feared falling into the void,
and how many times had you lowered the bascule?
Though the night casts uncertainty
every now and again,
I will remember seeing your soul at first sight—
the jewel star that guides me on.
So if your truth remains strong enough
to hold my sincerity I will make it to you,
come what may,
as you draw closer to me.
With each measured breath I reach for your love
and place it between us,
all the while holding it steadfast to mine.
For our new bridge knows
of no distance or separation—
its breadth unmeasured, its span but a vapor.

Morning Praise

I woke before the dawning light
to pause among the ancient stars, who
sing within the idle hours their sweet au bade
to daybreak. And while I sit upon this ridge, wrapped
in summer's fresh embrace—feeling life
stirring all around me—I think of all the
empty spaces within me.
The feats I have yet to master,
vibrant cities I long to explore,
the perpetual hunger to know myself more and more—
everything inside me,
unnamed and waiting,
keeps calling for me to continue my course.

As my mind reflects, it ponders on
the earthly span of a giant redwood
and her monumental years unfolding.
And soon a quiet composure settles easily inside me.
Her life, though not of one traversal,
her spirit reaches formidable heights—
while her limbs bend and wave on the wind,
she worships
the magnitude of existence in her own way. So I gather
my meandering thoughts
into a gentle hush to couple with this present,
seamless moment.

My chant softening alongside the early blear
is a silent song of praise for life and its complete
abundant merit.

We are all alive,
the trees, the stars, you and I,
and together we will sing into the morning eons.

Aligned

Does it matter if we meet on every level?
You first saw me as your antithesis,
not knowing I was bearing
your earliest wounds underneath
an aging smile. Never mind
that your hair has grayed softly,
or that the lines have deepened beside my eyes
as the years carried us toward one another.
Craving understanding, we finally recognized—
as if for the first time—
our beautiful reflection revealed, and in an open mirror
we share awareness.
It's all right that your clothes are worn in disarray
or that my scrambled words don't always make it to you
in the full context of their meaning—
for when we unveil our fears,
then release all the false ideals,
we embrace a clear perception
and become what is real and lasting.
And while I stumbled along in my own world
knowing you were in yours,
the days seemed so disheveled
without you in them—incomplete shambles.
Once joined, it all fell into place—
it grew to make perfect sense.

Will we need soft music coiling within seductive lighting
to climax into blissful realization?

Or can we soar to unimaginable heights
entwined in one another's eyes, encouraging our visions
into ripe, edible fruit to nourish us the rest of the way?
Will we remain enamored without the excess,
and not be swallowed up by life?
While we're captivated by the wondrous forest inside,
we learn there is so much more to explore,
with all the rest to uncover.
As we complement everyday living
with our most passionate desires
we stay wrapped around each other,
two vines climbing time—
my dreams 'round yours,
yours around mine.

Do you know what determines our bond
then keeps us affixed? And what
fused our soul connection?

What holds us is that you saw me
in my most vulnerable of moments,
and didn't turn away.
What melds us is that you genuinely placed your
innermost heart in my care,
and I kept it alive, nurturing it's every pulse, tenderly.
What matters in the design of love is this,
that two beings show themselves
to one another every day,
then ride out the storms
secured in the strength of their trusting embrace.
The sweet, resilient fastening between truth and love
is the most divine and sacred alignment.

Aerial Hawk

Now golden drops of light descend
upon the fairest blossom—still hours before
the evening star, she rounded out in wider rings.

Perched within an age-old forest, lifting
skyward and wildly confident—
alongside blue-clad winds, her flight an ancient song.

I'll come back this way—the next time around—
and join her swim with gliding circles,
through sovereign air
that holds our boundless callings.

And all the brokenness below us,
all the parted ones in sorrow,
an anxious world yet battle-torn,

will take comfort in our aerial psalm.
There is peace in the heart, despite all that rages,
there is peace as we sail through the storm.

Sugar Maples

He departed before the coldest of days arrived,
the world lay still in perfect slumber under glass—
and the pale frost sought to hide my inmost view.

While the wind grows brisk each night,
the fire inside keeps softly stirring—
so I sit and warm myself in reverie.

Though wrapped in early winter's chill,
autumn lingers fervently in my mind—
how the sugar maples burned with sweetness.

Soon the days will be stretching out for me,
and January's biding grip will gently melt in time,
as he recalls the night our hearts closed in.

His trust I'm earning now,
the road less treacherous than before—
when I loved him silently.

Home to Zion

I say you are my destination,
I see your vision wherever I roam.
I claim safe refuge in my Zion,
where my grief has been atoned.
Don't be afraid to hear, nor ever fear to know—
the eternal presence of my truth,
in you, my native home.

Lost Waves

Where do they go?
All the thoughts and ideas rushing in,
colliding with scattered sands,
defining lines
refining patterns,
concepts and plans—
coalescing in the mind,
inside yours, within mine.
Where do they go, all the thoughts outside lore?
Lost then forgotten in one single wave.
Do they recede back into time— in a sea of
possibility—
find their swell once again,
then wash up on a distant shore?

Inner Peace

Did I lie to you?
Did I appear as if I did not care?
Oh, if only you knew
how often I'd painted
you into all my solitary landscapes,
brightly fixed as the sun,
my centered one,
our beam warming
the many florets
within our devotion.

I was not a mere thought you conceived
or a doubtful whisper you once spoke aloud,
but a gentle song calling to you
ever softly in the night—
fluttering close to your slumbering ears,
then landing carefully into your dreams,
to be birthed into breathing life.

Often in the morning
I arrived as sweet light
to wake your senses,
remaining as the day to watch over you—
caressing you with the calming breeze,
and bathing you in a glow of serenity.

When in the moments of confusion
and despondency,
you wept for me—
I heard you.
So into your cry I came
to silence the fray within you,
and kiss your hungering heart
with the gifts of understanding.

And in between all our separations,
I imagined I could hear your breaths
among each one of my heartbeats,
as if our prayers had harmonized
somewhere in time and space—
blending voices
speaking a sole language,
echoing the love
only we recognize.

No, I did not lie to you.
I was always there,
quietly waiting
for our time.

Windstorm

There was a storm keeping me from sleep
one night, with thunder stomping
after each bolt, and the wind walloping
fiercely against the wall.
When the trembling earth reached out
to my foundation
in search of some secret hiding place,
I thought about the years in
passing, and all those who tried
to feed me their fear—how our struggle
lay inside my belly, still.
I felt an ache so visceral in my spirit when
recognizing this honest canvas we share.
Maybe I should have asked, what is it
that is making you so anxious?
Are you frightened in the night not knowing
what sits before you?
Do you fear a door opening,
the color from your dreams escaping,
or allowing that ardent comet within you
to fly open and free?
Do you worry you will not be courageous enough to
live your most bountiful life,
only to be ruined by all its hungry callings?
And are you afraid of the lightning within you
striking hope on fire,
then blazing all around you,

reducing you to magnificent hot coals
of lived out imaginings?

Now calm and undaunted I feel,
even in my windstorm.
How the truth, like gusts, draws near
to latch hold of my deepest rumblings,
urging me to live my bold and valiant life—
and not drift off to sleep, just yet.
I love the raging storm inside me.
It›s a mighty force within us all.

Love

Though I was formless,
you arrived from behind the hidden realm to shape me.
Though I was asleep,
you became the clearest light to wake me.
When I was alone,
you paced me alongside your footsteps,
that I might walk with you, always.
My heart was a blank sheet,
now you are the scribe who writes on it.

Ever Sweet

As September fades away
I sit listening to the pining crickets
give their melancholy call,
less urgent than before—
the last of the hopeful lovers
holding out for enchantment.
While summer's blithe and carefree spirit
is silently forgotten and
the fragile night of early autumn
closes in with cooler blues,
I'm reminded of all our gifted hours.
So I tuck away the twilight as a secret promise
for when I'm old and fading.
Though I'll not be as fresh
as our evening spent
or like the singing crickets
of summer's past,
I've the kiss in my memory
of you, ever sweet,
so the song of my youth
will last.

A Spiritual Life

A spiritual life is a ceaseless opening flower—
learning, stretching, giving, and being
alive with each new dawning,
welcoming all to its unfolding—
compassionate and aware
of wide surroundings,
sharing truth, and
with kindness,
offering
love.

Rivulet Tanka

Fanned, my rivulets
wait for you—wishes streaming,
layered, lingering—
forming all around you, in
ribbons of glossy dreaming.

I Could Have Been

I could have been
the wind
drifting by
a moonlit evening,
now vanishing.
Instead,
I could have been
a petaled lotus song—
opening up
then closing in,
rather than
an ancient sun
reaching out
to caress your skin,
as day goes by
a warming light,
timidly withdrawing.
I could have been
a falcon winged and
proudly circling
back around—
all at once,
transitioning
into a flow
of gentle feathers,
freshly falling to the ground.

I could have been
a towering mountain,
softening streams
winding through
majestic crags
of hardened scars
beneath the tender
drops of dew.
I could have been
a breath of air
inside each morning
born anew—
impassioned search
returning home,
to settle faintly
into you.
Then again,
I could have been.

Hope Is a Traveler

You step out of time
a weary traveler
from some other era
of another place—
looking worn and disheveled—
wearing shabby clothes
and a beautiful countenance.
All the miles between
that separate our embrace
now vanish in a sudden breath
outside your smile,
when suddenly the clock shatters
into shining timeless pieces
as you close the distance.

And I wonder where you came from—
no photographs or clippings tell
the birth of your infinite journey.
As you walk through the portal
of epochs passing,
you break the glass
which held the sands
and once confined my yearnings.

Radiance

I flourish in our light,
I laugh in your smile,
I sync with your eyes,
then close my own
to feel the radiance.

Trust Stars

I could have gazed endlessly at the stars above—
charmed crowd in the hollow black sky,
as they seduced and beguiled me, those
enthralling enchanters,
dressed up in their semblance of magic.
How many bright wishes had I cast out
into a thousand open nights,
only to be given an array
of bleak hope?
Until that one twilit evening
when you and I stood
outside any pretense,
with every illusory notion undressed
and bared—
clad only in the luster of faith,
where we became lost in a kiss,
and our trust shined like stars
that demystified
the darkness.

Cherry Blossom

Sunrise,
a cherry blossom folded.
Her scent drifts on the wind now,
remembering her sweetness,
as the sun sets tonight.

Celestial Moon

Nights are drawing in now,
the darkness is lonely for its glowing moon.
Even if the world grew silent tonight,
I'd think of you,
then hear your sweet song
play on in my heart.

O celestial moon,
how the vastness cries aloud for your return.
Without you, there is a loss among the heavens,
and this ocean of emptiness
fills with the tears
I sing.

Through Your Eyes I See

Your eyes view openly and strong,
sensing all times at once.
I behold their want to rest in beauty,
and perceive the nuances of life,
then see through all of the not life.

They want to mirror the miracle in true being—
they want to feel cherished.
In your eyes I see the infinite depth and perspective.

And through your eyes I see love clearer
than ever through my own.

Moonlight in Me

I sit beneath the darkened sky
fixed in reverential awe,
because of the moon—
in all its reflective splendor
above me revealing,
intently pouring
numen of light,
discerning all my intimate life longings,
while sharing her sweet mystery.

Well out and beyond
the length of night's vast and
lacquered canopy
there lies a hidden cross-way,
the point each world connects.
When we meet
at the deepest place in our hearts,
your heaven
fills my earth
and we are swept, entwining souls
rapt in glory.

I can't explain
its purpose grand,
or why it exists at all—or why the truth of me
dwells in you, so radiant,
like the moonlight shining
through all my darkest secrets.

Miles Between Us

Five hundred miles between us tonight,
I could walk them all,
and never back.
The road spread out before us,
steep hills of jagged cries
and cobbled stone—
all our fear and pain kept bound,
finally loosed and evanesce in time.
Every stronghold raised,
then bared—we held our breath and waited—
while the walls this life contrived
soon burned to the ground.
Always changing was your mind,
now solid earth beneath the sky.
Constant shifting, my terrain—
at last, safe and sound.
None to misgive, nor to falter—
drawing near and closing in,
holding fast to never wander,
but to share the same horizon
when your world melts into mine.

Fierce Jeweled River

Your mind is a
fierce jeweled river
swimming over
molten rocks,
nimbly flowing
ongoing torrent
melting my core.
Your voice is a waterfall
consumed by fire,
tender spills
dissolving my ears
into eyes alive,
watching wild flames soar.
Your soul is a strong
truth rooted,
white-pearled wisdom
guiding prism,
taking my hands,
holding deep
to love,
never asking
for more.

Hidden Words

Cradled tightly, never spoken,
words conceived do not emerge—
spring to life, yet never birth.
Collecting dust of sparking wonder,
hidden away in a secret cache,
with no sunlight to illuminate them,
or a wispy breath to penetrate them.

And when the world's in silent slumber,
I'll spill them out to admire each one—
try them on with my honeyed voice,
dancing and whirling about.
Oh, the splendor you'll miss out on—
when you told me to hide them away,
those words that I dare not say.

Companions

Courage took the hand
of timid visions and aspirations,
and together they crossed over
into a world of
creation.

On Happiness

I used to think it was better to not know the happiness
I could be missing out on.
And so I would evade it
whenever I felt it approach me,
because I feared loving it, then losing it.
Eventually, I imagined it went away,
and I became saddened.

I realized, finally, that it was meant for me to conceive
in this life,
and grow to well freely and abounding.

So happiness—I know who you are now,
you're a living spring in me—
and I know to hold on
and let go of you,
for however long
you stay.

The Song of Your Soul

As you sit day after passing day
on the outskirts of your own existence
wishing to be heard, wanting to be seen,
waiting to be touched—
do you feel the air of a certain unknown expectation
slowly leaking out from your heart?
Are you waiting internally,
while the edges of your soul quietly fold in?

Wherever you are in this world tonight,
within you plays a lasting song.
While the angels sing to God's delight,
the worthwhile beauty contained inside
your soul's melodious imprint
outperforms the celestial choir above.
And who you are at this very moment,
is so vital to who you will become.

For one day soon you will step into your own
stunning universe—beyond the myths,
outside any limitations or predictions,
far from the illusions this life invents—
as you answer the call to uncover
the many starlit truths contained inside
your incomparable soul.

You will be reborn to fresh and glorious revelations
only you can carry to completion.

And while all the infinite possibilities expand within,
may you sing aloud, rejoicing in your new birth,
no longer owned by anyone's idea
of who you should be.

Sweet Wine

The very first vision I had of you
was a sip of sweet wine to come.
Once, you and I shared love's journey,
then meeting in a halfway point we joined anew.

As we walked along the shoreline in a dream so
otherworldly, we allowed for love
to settle into all the spaces that we are,
then splash over into life.

In your palms were many revelations,
in your eyes so many more.
Each day I tell you of my fervent desire,
my longing to be near.
And when there is nothing left for me to confess,
after you lift the final veil,
I will go to you
with all my body.

Orchard of My Being

I understand not everything in its entirety, yet
it is enough for each day to satisfy.
Within me there is a waiting harvest—
inside me, many trees.
Trees so strongly rooted
from years gone by, their limbs
ready to stretch now, with anticipating wonder,
with ripe fruit to make sense of,
to fill a hungry bushel.
All in my own time, I'll gather the yield—all within
my own terrain.
Unknown perceptions, finally seeing—
where sage blooms grow
complete and profound—
in prolific musing,
creation abounds.
I'll collect among this endless bounty,
from the orchard of my being.

Quest

Take me past
the guarded place
in you
where confusion
covers itself
in unrelenting confidence,
then marches on
in lively steps.
Take off the façade,
let it fall away
into nowhere.
Turn around and face me.
I search the infinite depth,
where beyond all entrenchments
I find your thirst
to be met
and understood,
the sadness in your bones,
the want of your silent cries
to be heard
and be known—
abiding within those
unseen landscapes,
is a world of precious dreams.
Let me touch where
the battle wounds
lie quietly healing.

Buried beneath
an armored sheath
rests a lifetime of love
and loneliness,
blame and triumph,
honor and defeat.
Within this blended web
of scars and treasures,
glistening with honesty,
there you are—
I found you,
beneath the soldier's plated heart.
So loosen the knots around my own,
see all its agony bared and mending,
and in between each open space
we'll breathe upon the frailty.
All the wishful longings to be had
bring to me yours,
as I meet you there with mine.

Breathless

Though the sea rushes forth
washing away sands before,
still clinging to you,
I am breathless.

While life's misty shadows
dance upon the shore,
still watching for you,
I wait, restless.

I Wondered

I wondered as a child,
where did the wind go
after it passed me by,
how long will a star burn
before it dies,
where did the dawn wait—`
and will there ever be arms to hold me?

As I sat on the shore of midlife,
my spirit as tremendous
as the inexhaustible lake before me—
I felt my destiny afire,
ready to meet a world to come.
And I wondered, right then,
will my body be enough to hold me?

Forever Blue

What they say
about your eyes,
clearing skies
shining through—
in those watercolor seas
a twilight breeze,
getting lost,
finding hope
within the vivid hue.
What they say
I didn't see, in those
colors deeply true—
but ethereal light
of loving souls
and peace
surrounding you.
I saw decision
eclipse confusion—
seeing all that was before,
then all that would ensue.
I saw you reach for
something more,
I saw me
inside the blue.

A Single Leaf

A single leaf,
so tenuous yet persevering,
even after its falling.
A single leaf,
solitarily drifting
atop an ageless stream,
no longer attached—letting go,
to be carried along by the tender white current.
A single leaf, within it
tells the story of an entire season.

Solitude

In the stillness of being alone,
hear the inner voice revealing.
Allow the moment of solitude
to hold you in safe trust,
and be not afraid of its teachings.
In the quiet sunrise live a million loving sermons.
Within a field of golden wild grass
the subtle light of faith unfurls a new day's
opening psalm.
In this sole moment, unique while you are in its care,
you are by yourself, though not ever alone.
As its gentle notes guide your listening heart
to come back to yourself,
hear this music
others call silence.

Only the Heart Road

I'm swept by soothing waves of gratitude
washing gently through my spirit, and it feels
much like grace has summoned it right on time.
It's best when it arrives this way, and not be
pressed through falsely. It's cleansing when
sorrow is allowed to weep, while compassionate
to loosen the grip of anger.

So when a blessing like this appears—
a cut inflicted long ago,
urgently tucked away as heartache, finally surfacing
as clear and unexpected cries for restoration—
only the heart road is the path to take.
All other routes lead on to dead ends,
and the only option is to walk
in healing strides.

On the Road of Great Wonder

Once in a while they'll remind you
how you could have been someone great,
or could have accomplished a noble feat—if only.
What is greatness?
Is it that you want to pave a vast road of achievements
that will cover all of time
with your works and your namesake?
The greatest derive from humble beginnings—
they begin by simply being.
Dormant yet alive, they embark on the greatest voyage
holding tightly to dreams and visions, hoping
one day to break their shell and push out from the dirt.
As they labor and plod along,
they feel the heat of the day
warm their dewy skin,
beyond the mire of worry.
Their fragrance, never wasted, goes out into the wind
offering salt to each new morning, as imperfect grains
enhancing the entire day around them.
Through it all, despite it all, they persevere
because they learned over and over
that the splinters of disappointment
can emerge as paragons of victory
as they knit their great, intricate uniqueness.

On they walk, in spite of all the harsh taskmasters—
naysayers casting gloom, critics finding fault,
accusers inciting blame,
and through every shaming obstacle.
With each honorable step moving forward,
watching life unfold with marvel,
as beings simply being, they walk
upon this pathway of great wonder.

And the road is plenty wide and welcoming,
speaking out to all,
This is the perfect place,
this is the right time,
this is where wish becomes possible.

Once Before

*H*e was the first I saw that year,
before I saw myself completely,
and I stepped quietly into his arms.

He was in a dream once before,
as he held my every unspoken desire,
I stepped trustingly into his arms.

Tourmaline Seas

I miss your eyes most of all,
calm tourmaline seas.

In them I can see an endless bliss,
so heavenly and lasting.

That feeling I get, as if eternity were
prompting me to join your love with mine,

keeps me longing for yet another glimpse.
Once fixed upon their joyous depths,

I sink below the fathoms. And your eyes,
like soulful oceans, confirm my deepest need.

Endless Woods

If it became quiet
in your endless woods,

and all you could hear
was the silence of a hushed wind,

while the trees stood soundless and still
among the muted thicket—

the song thrush in its dormant sleep,
not even the whisper of an insect,

with the winding brook
no longer ruminating or reflecting—

if you came to discover
that the expression you once sought

and grew to know,
had somehow vanished,

would the absence make you mourn,
then search for that voice

as a thirsty hart in quest of an uttering stream?
And if you found it again,

would you cherish it this time?
Would you tend and nurture it—

until it flowered, then
make way for its power

letting it bloom over and again,
stretching out into the open air,

filling the entire space around you—
waking life back from its quiescent rest,

this spirited voice
in your endless woods.

River

It never seemed important that anyone
should read the story of my journey.
Only, I read it again this evening
and wanted to tell you,
there are lines which never fail to describe
my feeling for breath and adventure,
or the unexpected draw that pulls our lives to such
astonishing confluence right on time.

And in the spaces before you—all those glorious
moments held in many
different pockets—I lived wildly daring
as a gypsy exploring,
inhaling all the beckoning calls to roam,
splashing in unseen fortune along the way.
I lived wary and peaceful, being careful and still,
enfolded in soil and
resting on earth as her spirits
passed down timeless guidance.
I live truthful with passion, honoring my days in praise
of being, while moving onward.

So if they ever do read it—and get to the part
of the river that takes us—they'll read of its sweeping
through hours and lands,
sharing weakness then strength
over rugged terrain and softening hillsides.

They'll read of your story,
which fell beside mine—
how they tangled and writhed, fervidly flowing,
running twists and calms, then finally merging as one
blending essence.

And this stream wells forth continually,
carrying us sweetly
into the deepest swells of the ocean,
within the truest heart of our knowing.

Cryptic Lines

Sometimes we feel we're brazen lovers,
sometimes coy, like timid children,
sometimes we laugh as old friends—
and at times it's as though we did it all once before,
while it feels we haven't even scratched the surface.
We've yet to decipher the code of our fated path.
I read you and feel my perplexity
form like cryptic lines
I must try to untangle—
and then you smile at me.

Far away from this temporal world,
where time is ceaseless, we are immortals.
I saw life as endless flowers
in an infinite field of sunlight.
My traveled soul holds a secret confidence,
my covered face hides an ancient scholar,
my timorous heart is a marveled teller
of myth and fortune, fame and legend.
Tales of gods and Egyptian kingdoms,
of tattooed wrists with Coptic symbols,
elephant seals on a sandy beach,
the jeweled Pyrenees and blue waters, deep—
starlit nights when I could not sleep,
but think about my faraway home, how
without its heart, I felt alone.

Your gentle face is a shining lantern,
your open soul is a guide of truth,
your wounded heart is a steady healer—
casting light in countless blessings
for all the broken unbelievers.
Writing lines of hallowed wisdom
on the walls of soulful dreamers,
with your sacredness disheveled,
you are poised in chaotic beauty.
Giving riches from your bounty
as you walk in tattered threads,
you've a crown upon your head—
you're the prince of inner peace,
offering man's apology.

And I,
so hollowed by doubt yet filled with dreams,
crushed into dust, but like diamonds still gleam—
calling on you to come for me now
and bring me back home,
so I might live them out.
Then you smile at me.
A smile that transcends words,
yet speaks a dozen complicated languages.
And you,
you are the Scribe of cryptic lines.

Starling

*I*f this heart of mine
could last forever
inside the starling's
morning call,
to rise above
the trees and higher
and death my flight
should not befall.
This heart of mine
would soar forever,
enraptured in
a timeless song—
as day is born
my heart is calling
for you, my wind,
to sing along.

Idyll Moon

*I*n bed at night,
you, with your hair tousled
between my fingers,
nestled inside my softness,
you fill
so well—
sprouting my sigh,
lips touching
each ripple,
cresting soon—
then I bend to kiss
your warm skin,
as the moon sits idly by.

Grain of Sand, Flower, Star

Grain of sand, flower star,
born of an ancient quasar.
Bold and bright,
numinous light,
powerful energy ignite.
Infinite line never begins
and knows no end—
descending kin
joining paths
of sinuous course,
to fade or fall away, perforce.
Circle round,
meet in position
with no extension,
yet connecting by transition.
Cycles in motion,
relations woven,
threads pulled, warp and curve—
celestial cloth bends and swerves.

Grain of sand, flower, star—
defined, then named
who you are.
Sharing time, space and earth,
each one contributes to its worth.
Millions within billions quantified, and
perpetuate, when multiplied—
then weave through time
a majestic shawl,
covering
all.

Inspiration

When the days were veiled in darkness
and all I could feel was the cold slate of my sadness,
you came to me like a season,
subtly changing everything.
While the shadows slowly melt away,
your light reaches out to me.
Awakening thought
rains as a cleansing,
imparting revelation's sweet fragrance
to imbue deep within me.
Then shining outward,
my true voice,
a symphony—
and flowers, now in song,
where once was a field
that faded
in silence.

Crystal Pool

I loved you back then—
did you see it begin?
I saw you in a crystal pool,
then plunged right in.
I still tremble when you call to me—
what am I to do?
Always wanting to dive in
and stay on,
loving you.

Our Song

Last night I heard the song we made,
its soothing notes drift on the air—
through slumbering dance
our souls joined truth,
and the darkened winds could not pervade
this gentle chorus light we share.

Image

All my life I chased God's image
to confirm my own existence,
all my life I sought God's
spirit to be explained.
Until I looked inward.
Every fiber, every strand
held the glory of I Am—
and as the truth of me unveiled,
the richest depth of me then surfaced.
God's divinity
and my humanness
are the same.

The Secret of Hope

Can I tell you of a secret shared between you and me?
The worldly possessions, the career, the accolades—
the things that can be bought and sold,
do not matter to us at all.
The negative energy from someone's parting words has
no real power over our destiny.
The uncertain circumstances of an unsettling childhood
cannot deter us when it has lost its final stronghold,
its grip weakening
with each forward step.
For we are all wounded children
finding our way to loving parents—
and somehow we'll manage to find them, somewhere,
to fill the love-bare rooms inside.
Even within us they wait, arms wide open.

Without seeing,
without knowing,
we ache for something so vastly extraordinary
with every part of our being, silently weeping,
until our tears speak aloud
our greatest longing.
And like a desperate prayer of petition
we vow to make good
in exchange for that great need to be answered,
so the pain of this wanting
might be quelled and soothed.

Without seeing,
without knowing,
the secret is, more than anything, we want to give.
We want to live imparting hope, so it will never perish.
And because we carry hope alive within us
and offer it without cost,
we are so vastly extraordinary,
well beyond our greatest longings.

Cornflower

Each day a storm of darkened clouds,
to water down and dampen dreams.
I have a pensive mind tonight, fraught with worry
against the blue. Refusing to be discouraged
by layering gloom clouds,
I shelter my spirit in each day's renewing promise.

And I think about a cornflower—
somewhere in a morning field,
far away from here—singing out
to the sky's vermillion sunrise,
with not a care in the world.

Sacred Marriage

See the rose in bloom,
its essence even more graceful
when seen through the eyes of purity.
Before the early mist rises,
deep in the heart of hearts,
each petal falls away
to reveal a priceless pearl.
Melting within this beauty,
transmuted by love divine—
I alone am yours,
and you, my soul,
are mine.

Oceans Deep

You and I,
it seems
we've more to reap—
beyond boundaries,
transcending time,
and oceans deep.
Spiraling down
a thousand leagues,
we are immersed.
For you are the burning
I caught fire to,
and I am the quench
that sates your
urgent thirst.

The Stream

*H*e said it doesn't exist inside an immaculate room.
It does not pour out from an open chakra.
It can't be birthed within the sweetest of incense,
in the past or present samsara spaces—
or found in the center of mystic places.
It is not in the cymbal's chime,
not in a cache of secret wealth,
not hidden inside laws of esoteric traditions
nor written in the holiest of scripture text.

It is here, on this plane,
in this realm
and routine—
it is the cooling ford from an open ravine.
It is the all-knowing and seeing,
formed by the prayers and unspoken devotion
of those who came before.
Each time we draw near, hear it reminding
of the divinity within each living thing.

For we are all testaments of truth
near the ancient stream—
meant for you, accessible to me.
So let us approach and immerse freely,
for however long
and deep.

About the Author

Susan Frybort is an American-born poet with a deep fascination for life and the human experience. Writing since she was a child, her poems are a tapestry of wisdom and compassion that soften the heart's edges, calling us home. Previously published in Elephant Journal and Vivid Life, 'Hope is a Traveler' is her first formal collection. Her beautiful hearticulations can also be read in author Jeff Brown's novel 'An Uncommon Bond', as the poetic voice of the female lover. Susan is also a skilled tailor, whose interests include astronomy and nature exploration. She is a proud mother to her daughter, Lindsay.